This
B-baLL book
BeLONGS to

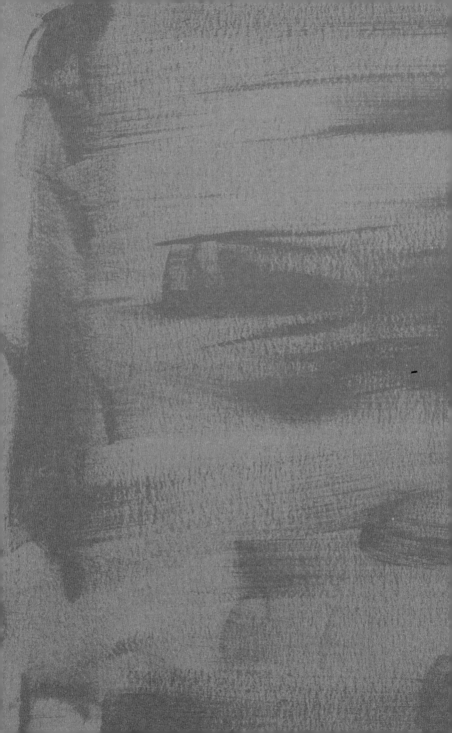

To Sophie,

Dreams + Drive = Success

[signature]

3/12

HOOP

*Dedicated to lovers of the game,
who appreciate it in all its forms*
—*C. R. S. Jr.*

Kings

Poems by
**Charles R.
Smith Jr.**

CANDLEWICK PRESS

CONTENTS

Allen
Iverson

Crooked cornrows
cause chaotic
and catastrophic collisions
with precision.
Your mission
  and goal:
    put the ball
      in the hole
using lightning-quick speed
and total body control.
Tattooed warrior
sinking shots legendary
putting up points
by any means necessary.
Crossover is nice,
   defenses get sliced
     like cheese,
opponents freeze
as you do what you please
with ease

like step back
and drain threes
   or blow
        into the lane
like a hurricane breeze.
No fear
No shame
drives your
one-hundred-sixty-five-pound
     body
       and
          six-foot frame
like a lightning bug
        zig-zaggin'
that can't be
contained.
Your name
draws defenders
like moths to a flame
     and scorches opponents
        with heat all the same.

By ANY MEANS
NECESSARY

Up high
down hard
orange orbs **blast**
through silken nets
like hammers through **glass**
smashin' mediocrity
with authority
and
aerial artistry
causin' simple
Vinsanity.
Number 15
doing his thing
running **hard**
fanning **wide**
on the right wing,
legs pump-pump-pump
for takeoff
ready to lift off
over runway
of wide eyes
and extended arms
for a big sendoff.
Wings **soar** into clouds
drawin' rain
on airplane
windowpanes
from atmosphere
to stratosphere

ready to
bring the pain
with agility
power
and grace
when VC drops
like an asteroid on fire
from the deep
deep reaches of space
with a one-handed
windmill three-sixty
power jam
IN YOUR FACE!

OUT OF THIS WORL

Vince
Carter

MONE
iN TH
BA

All-natural skills
spring from fundamental drills,
banking off the glass.

Leather bumps backboard
from geometric angles,
banking off the glass.

Inside and outside,
right side and left side, always
banking off the glass.

Smooth seven-footer
cashes in double digits,
banking off the glass.

Tim
Duncan

ILL skills
cause **shakes**
shivers
and **chills**
from crossover thrills
with the pill
when the Franchise Flu
strikes.

Fever-induced heat
wears out
ligaments
and feet
causing cough-ups
on **D**
when the Franchise Flu
strikes.

Infectious dunks
over seven-foot chumps
cause **aches**
and **pains**
and muscular **strains**
when the Franchise Flu
strikes.

Mind-numbing
throat-soring
outrageously **sick**
game of Steve Francis
spreads contagiously quick
when the Franchise Flu
strikes.

WILL

Steve
Francis

IN

Kevin
Garnett

Analog amateurs analyze
three-dimensional game
from frame
of snake's-eye view
when KG goes
double digital
throwing triple statistical
skills at you
hit-
   hit-
      hittin'
twos from every
inconceivable angle
causing three-dimensional

DAMAGE

to your game
when the KG Mainframe
goes
di-
   di-
      digital.

Laserlike line-drive passes
lead to lazy lay-ups
off shiny Plexiglas
when KG goes
di-
   di-
      digital.

Air balls
bricks
clinks
clanks
and clunks
are cleaned up
as KG puts back
all the junk,
polishing Plexi with
frequency
when he goes
di-
   di-
      digital.

Teeth ch-ch-ch-chatter
from devastatingly disastrous
dunks
that shatter backboards in
stere-
   ere-y-
      O
when KG goes
di-
   di-
      digital
playing
triple-dimensional
basketball **Y2KG STYLE.**

WhaT'S iN A NaMe?

SOLE SHOWN ACTUAL SIZE

*S*uper

*H*uman

*A*tomic

*Q*uake

Jason
Kidd

Breaking fast
while speeding past,
stop-sign defenders
quick as a *flash,*
Accelerator accelerates
toward checkered flag.
Engine shifts into overdrive
riding over barriers
for
2 more
points
1 more
board
and assist,
zoom
zoom
zooming
in
for the swish.

License plate:
TRPL DBL
spinning circles
around the track
to the rack,

shifting speeds
from super
to sonic
to hyper
to **light.**
Model JK32:
with legs of **dynamite**
explodes on court with style,
speed,
and flair,
exhausts competition,
leaves them **gasping for air.**

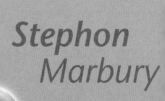

Stephon
Marbury

Buckle up
keep your hands inside
  as the Coney Island Cyclone
   takes you on a ride
    when Starbury strides
    and spins
    on soles
    in control
    on clickety-clack tracks
    headed straight for the rack
    with a
           CRACK!
    of ankles snapping back.
    Cyclone swerves wide
   on swirling dribble drives
  shifting tracks
         from right
     to left
 o left

        to right
      switching up
       speeds
        from h e s i t a t i o n
        to
            outasight,
       storming through trees
       whipping passes like leaves
       dropping long-distance
       threes,
        tomahawk-dunk chopping
        opponents to knees
       as they beg
       and whimper
       and pray
       and plead:
       PLEASE, PLEASE, PLEASE
       MAKE IT STOP!

THE
YCLONE

Come one
come all

to witness Basketball Theater
featuring Tracy McGrady
as the
Innovator
Crowd Captivator
Multiple Category
    Statistic Generator.
Assist Manipulator
Rebound Accumulator
The Now-You-See-Me
Now-You-Don't
    Dribble Drive Creator,
Shot-Fake
    Exploding-to-the-Hole
        Accelerator.
Offense Orchestrator

Defense Infiltrator
High-Flying
Shot-blocking
    Fast-Break Activator,
Eagle-Eye Ball-Snatching
    Pass Confiscator.
Paint Penetrator
Base-line Skater
Six-Eight
    Long and Lean
        Air Levitator,
Hovering-over-Heads
        Helicopter Aviator.
Coast-to-Coast
    Obstacle Course Navigato
Flying-Through-the-Lane
    Finger-Roll Fascinator.
Opponent Agitator
3-Point Detonator
Equal Opportunity
    Embarassment Educator

*T-Mac in the spotligh
blinding spectators!*

ONE-
MAN
SHOW

24

Tracy
McGrady

VELVET HAMMER

Chris Webber

Strong smooth skills
score from swift-shaking shoulders,
showcasing spectacular spins.

Feathery fingertips
flick fadeaways
from far away
with flair.

Relentless reflexes
rattle rising rebounds
into rigid rims.

Fine-tuned fundamentals
focus ferocious fire,
fueling force and finesse.

MAZING

STEP RIGHT UP
AND HURRY ON IN.
THE AMAZING JASON
IS ABOUT TO BEGIN!

*Jason
Williams*

SEE

Abracadabra assists
POOF into 2-point tricks
with sleight-of-hand skill
by the Magnificent Magician
known as J-Will.

SEE

Presto-change-o
behind-the-back
ball fakes
move with magic touch
from cuff to cup
to finish off fast breaks.

SEE

Hocus-pocus highlights
materialize
before your very eyes
when between-the-leg dribble drives
vaporize
defenders into dust.

SEE

3-point illusions
baffle your mind
when toes are behind
the arc
and spark
long-distance matches,
lighting a torch
to scorch
nylon nets.

THE AMAZING JASON
PERFORMING IN PRIME TIME,
SO STEP RIGHT UP, FOLKS—
IT'S . . . SHOWTIME!

Kobe
Bryant

Creative and cool
confident moves
paint basketball masterpieces
from hip-hop grooves
on hardwood canvas
using bold brush strokes
of a bouncing ball.
Quicksilver spins blur
into indigo jump shots
accented by
purple dribble drives
SPLASHED
with high-flyin'
heart-stoppin'
eye-poppin'
jaw-droppin'
gravity-defyin'
fiery-red
DUNKS
that pump
LOUD
into the crowd.

When KB breaks out his palette
to skywalk on clouds,
becoming
the **POSTERizer**
POINT Emphasizer
The Hurry-Up-and-Hustle-Back
Shot **Vaporizer**
Crowd **Energizer**
In-the-Air Improviser
serving up
sizzling shake-and-break
appetizers,
sketching out masterpieces
with the touch of an artist's hand
using the ball as his paintbrush,
KB's **ALWAYS** in command.

PoeM NotEs

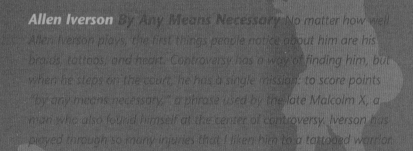

Allen Iverson **By Any Means Necessary** No matter how well Allen Iverson plays, the first things people notice about him are his braids, tattoos, and heart. Controversy has a way of finding him, but when he steps on the court, he has a single mission: to score points "by any means necessary," a phrase used by the late Malcolm X, a man who also found himself at the center of controversy. Iverson has played through so many injuries that I liken him to a tattooed warrior.

Vince Carter **Out of This World** For Vince Carter, I tried to use a description that was literally out of this world. I transformed Carter from a person into an asteroid that's picking up speed, ready to turn on its trajectory and smash into something down on Earth—in this case, the basketball rim.

Tim Duncan Money in the Bank Tim Duncan relies on fundamental, not flashy, moves. But this doesn't mean he can't get the job done. He can rack up twenty points and make it look easy. His "money shot," the one he relies on, is a short jump shot off the backboard. Since his game is traditional, I used four sets of haiku to describe him. The haiku is a Japanese poetry form that has three unrhymed lines: the first line has five syllables, the second has seven, and the last has five. I also played with words to show him "cashing in" his money shot at the bank.

Steve Francis ILL at Will Every time I've seen Steve Francis play, I've always found myself saying how "sick" he is. That's a slang word for intense and good. Even though he's six foot three, I've seen him dunk many times over much taller players. I asked myself what would make someone "sick" and came up with the flu, and since his nickname is Stevie Franchise, I just used all of the symptoms to describe someone catching the Franchise flu.

Kevin Garnett KG in 3D Standing at six feet eleven inches, yet performing with the versatility of someone much smaller, KG is a new breed of player. He does things that people his size normally just do not do. I call his game digital because it shows a new and improved way of doing things, just as digital technology is better than the old analog technology. Garnett's game is changing the way basketball is played for all players, big and small.

Shaquille O'Neal What's in a Name? What else is there to say about someone who stands more than seven feet tall, weighs over three hundred pounds, and dominates the game? I decided to focus on his unique name to describe these traits in a few simple words. The trick was choosing four words that would provide the biggest punch. This style of poem is called an acrostic and is often used to introduce newcomers to poetry because of its simplicity.

Jason Kidd Accelerator The point guard runs the show on offense and is sometimes called the spark plug that makes the team's engine go. Point guard Jason Kidd is like a racecar. Very fast on the court, he is also one of the few players who regularly gets a triple double—that's ten or more points in three statistical categories, such as points, rebounds, and assists. I also gave him a license plate (TRPL DBL) and a model number (JK32). Together they mean Jason Kidd, triple double.

Stephon Marbury The Cyclone Stephon Marbury is from Coney Island, New York, where there is a roller coaster called the Cyclone. Having lived in Brooklyn myself, I have been on the roller coaster, and it is a thrilling ride. I liken Stephon Marbury to the ride because he is a thrilling player who takes your breath away.

Tracy McGrady One-Man Show *Basing my rhyme scheme on the suffix "–ator" (meaning someone who does), I chose as many words as I could find to describe the unlimited potential and skill of Tracy McGrady and his complex, ever-evolving game.*

Chris Webber Velvet Hammer *I've watched Chris Webber play since college, and although he is a big guy with lots of power, he always has had a very light touch when taking a jump shot. On the basketball court, that translates into power and finesse—a velvet hammer.*

Jason Williams The Amazing *It was very easy for me to imagine Jason Williams as a magician because he makes the ball disappear on a regular basis. When I went to the circus as a kid, I enjoyed hearing the "barker" shout out who was performing, so I wrote the poem in that voice.*

Kobe Bryant The Creator *I am originally from Los Angeles and a die-hard Laker fan. Kobe Bryant is my favorite player. He has created shots on the basketball court that I have NEVER seen before. This is why I called him the Creator—I liken him to a painter, using different moves like different colors to form a masterpiece on the court.*

Growing up in Los Angeles, I remember watching Lakers games on television with my mother. We would be glued to the set as Magic Johnson, Kareem Abdul-Jabbar, Julius Erving, George Gervin, and other great players performed at the highest level with style and grace. Witnessing Magic throw no-look passes or Dr. J (Julius Erving) fly through the air for dunks, I thought: This is poetry in motion.

Watching these great players inspired me to perfect my jump shot, and I ran countless sprints to build up my legs, hoping one day to be able to dunk. While learning about basketball, I also started writing poetry. My first poems were simple "roses are red" poems for my friends, but as my game improved, so did my writing. Little did I know that these two loves would merge later in life.

Years later, after graduating from college and still playing ball, I have found myself writing children's books about the game I've grown up with and always loved. This book is a tribute to the players who make the game fun to watch. Thanks to all their new and exciting moves, I'm proud to say that to me, basketball is still "poetry in motion."

First paperback edition 2007

The Library of Congress has cataloged the hardcover edition as follows:

Library of Congress Catalog Card Number 2003055340

ISBN 978-0-7636-1423-2 (hardcover)

ISBN 978-0-7636-3560-2 (paperback)

SCP 15 14 13 12 11 10
10 9 8 7 6 5 4 3

Printed in Humen, Dongguan, China

This book was typeset in Stone Sans.

Digital artwork and typography by Caroline Lawrence

Candlewick Press, 99 Dover Street, Somerville, Massachusetts 02144

visit us at www.candlewick.com